Jack Gives Back

Stewardship Jack Series, Book **1**

by Janice Mathews

Review&Herald®

REVIEW AND HERALD PUBLISHING ASSOCIATION
SINCE 1861 | WWW.REVIEWANDHERALD.COM

Copyright © 2012 by North American Division Stewardship Ministries

Published by Review and Herald® Publishing Association, Hagerstown, MD 21741-1119

Review and Herald® titles may be purchased in bulk for educational, business, fund-raising, or sales promotional use. For information, e-mail SpecialMarkets@reviewandherald.com.

The Review and Herald® Publishing Association publishes biblically based materials for spiritual, physical, and mental growth and Christian discipleship.

Cover design by Ron Pride/Review & Herald Design Center
Interior design by Wendy Hunt/Plum Nelly Productions
Photos by Janice Mathews, Gary Eldridge (pp. 9, 12, 25), and Joseph Collins (pp. 19, 29)

Sponsored by:
North American Division Stewardship Ministries
General Conference Stewardship Ministries
North American Division Children's Ministries
General Conference Children's Ministries

PRINTED IN U.S.A.

16 15 14 13   5 4 3 2

Library of Congress Cataloging-in-Publication Data
Mathews, Janice, 1954-   .
Jack gives back / Janice Mathews.
p. cm. – (Stewardship Jack series ; bk. 1)
ISBN 978-0-8280-2667-3
1. Christian stewardship–Juvenile literature. 2. Tithes–Juvenile literature. I. Title.
BV772.M386 2012
248'.6--dc23
                                                     2012015604

ISBN 978-0-8280-2667-3

Introduction

The Stewardship Jack series is a set of books for children, preschool through second grade, on the topic of stewardship. These books are presented in a whimsical manner, using Jack, a goldendoodle, who has become "Stewardship Jack."

Plans are to have future books designed to attract the attention of children to other important topics about stewardship and to engender a positive regard for the care and use of the resources God has given.

Let me introduce Stewardship Jack (who absolutely loves people):

Stewardship Jack is a pup, black and furry;
He really can't talk, but gives "advice" to my query.
Willingly, Jack gives his affection to me,
Which reminds me of lessons from Malachi 3.

— Janice Mathews

In a text in the Bible-Malachi 3, verse 10—

God asks us to return the tithe, and then

He'll be happy to send special blessings our way;

He wants us to prove Him . . . Jack, what do you say?

Should I give the tithe back, Jack?

God gives us so much and asks only a little,
It's foolishly selfish even to quibble.

If returning a tithe brings a blessing from God,

Then not doing so would seem rather odd.

Tithing would seem like a most simple thing . . .

If you knew what it was and what you should bring.

How do you give a tithe back, Jack?

"Tithe" is a little–but important–word
If you don't know what it means, it's time that you heard.

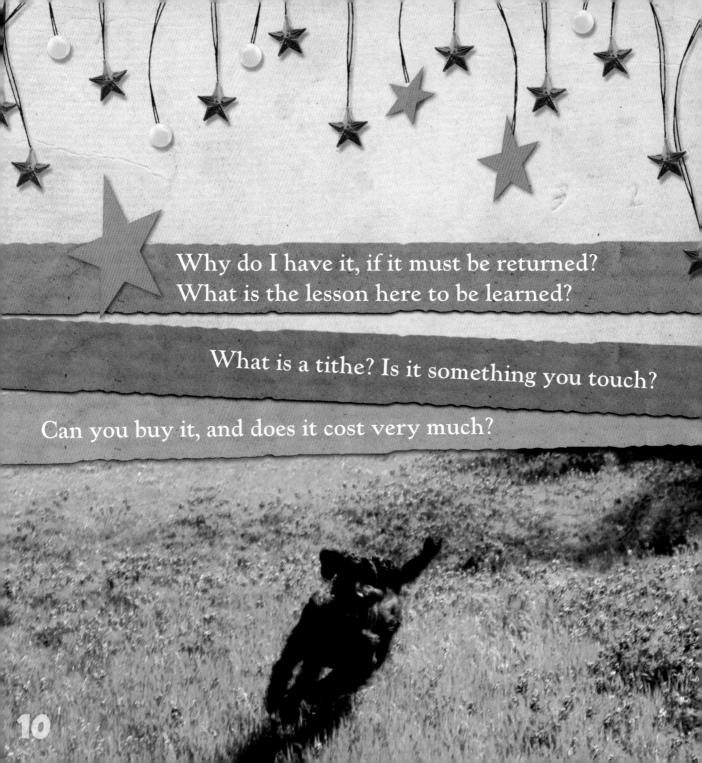

Why do I have it, if it must be returned?
What is the lesson here to be learned?

What is a tithe? Is it something you touch?

Can you buy it, and does it cost very much?

What is a "tithe" to give back, Jack?

A tithe is one tenth of all your increase;
A small part like that is easy to release.

I want houses and cars

and lots of toys!

Leave all the giving

to those girls and boys.

I work so hard and don't have enough.

Why should I give God any of my stuff?

13

Why should I give back, Jack?

God made the world, man, money, and dogs.
Let's manage like good stewards and not be like hogs.

It's hard to let go of all that God gives

When thinking from a selfish perspective.

What if I don't tithe—what happens then?

Is it really terrible? Is it a sin?

What if I don't give back, Jack?

God says it's like robbers who break in to steal.
If we take what is His, think how sad He must feel!

Abraham gave tithe to Melchizedek.

(To take them to him I'd have quite a trek!)

He lived long ago near Old Jerusalem;

He's no longer there, so how could I get it to him?

Where should I give it back, Jack?

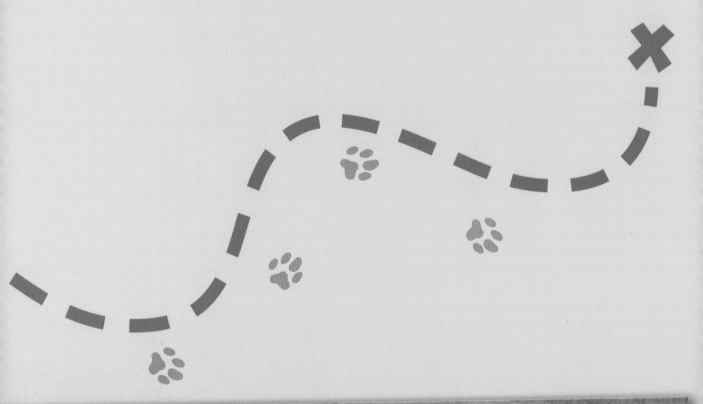

God wants it brought to His storehouse, the church.
You can find all that out by a Scripture search.

Jacob gave tithe of sheep, goats, and cattle.

If those were at church, there'd be a rodeo battle!

If I must tithe with goats, cattle, and sheep–

I have none of those, so my stuff I can keep?

What should I give back, Jack?

 A tithe is one out of every 10 that you gain.
Most of us gain money, so that is quite plain.

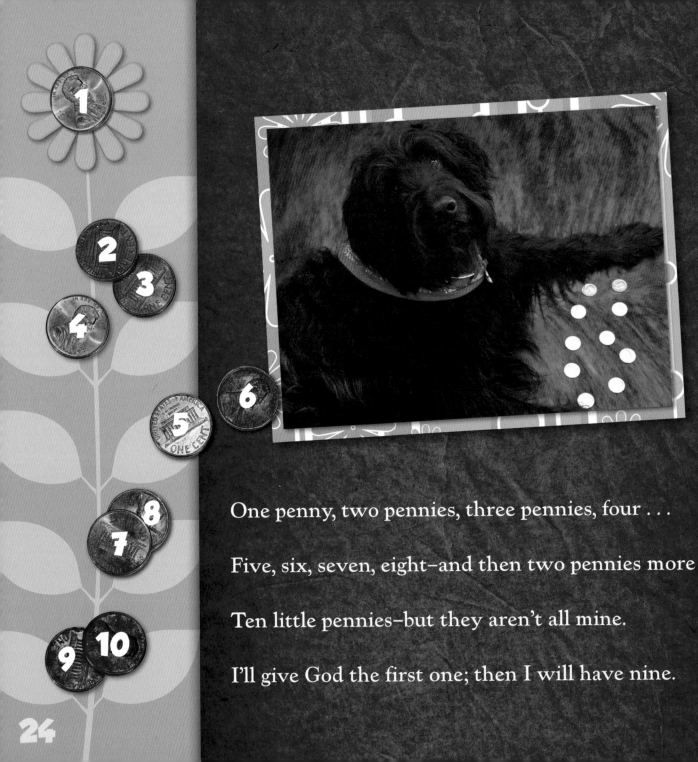

One penny, two pennies, three pennies, four . . .

Five, six, seven, eight—and then two pennies more

Ten little pennies—but they aren't all mine.

I'll give God the first one; then I will have nine.

Is this how I should give back, Jack?

A tithe is one out of every 10 that you gain: Coins, bones, or dollars—you should treat all the same.

If I gain 10 dollars [bones] and have lots of expenses,
I still give one to God—no straddling of fences.

There are nine whole dollars [bones] left, you see,
And a happy little steward I will be!

A happy and grateful steward will bring

Extra to give as an offering.

God's tithe is one out of every 10;

Your offering shows your thanks to Him.

All we have is God's, I know.

When I give to Him, my love I show.

I want to be a cheerful giver,

And His rich blessings God will always deliver!

You're a good learner for a human, you know.
My work here is done, so I guess I will go!

Parents, now you have the pleasure of activity time as you discuss *Jack Gives Back* with your child. The following activities and puzzles will make learning fun! Because they reflect the interests and abilities of different age levels, you can select those that work best for your family. Have fun learning about God and His blessings and love!

Bible Text: Malachi 3:10, first part.

This verse says that God wants us to bring our tithe to the storehouse.

Question: What is a tithe?

Answer: A tithe is *one* out of every 10.

A Tithe Is a Tenth . . . But How Much Is *That?*

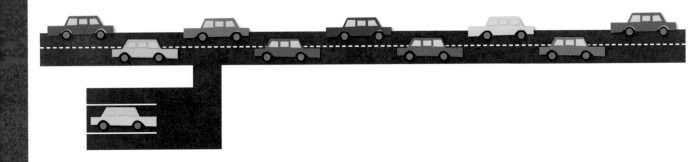

Materials: Gather 10 items (10 toy cars, 10 blocks, 10 balls, or 10 crayons, etc.).

Activity: Ask your child to count them, then take out one out of every 10 and set it aside. Call it a *tithe*. Point out that they still have nine items remaining.

Discussion: How do you give a tithe to God?

One for God, and Nine for Me

Materials: Your child's bank, 10 dimes, and a tithe envelope.

Activity: Help your child count the dimes, then set one dime aside for the tenth, or tithe.

Have your child write their name on the tithe envelope, and mark "10 cents" where it says "tithe."

Count together as the child puts the other nine dimes into a bank that they can keep. Before all the dimes are put into the bank, tell them that they can put extra into the envelope for offering, if they choose.

Suggestions: Your child's allowance can be given in both coins and bills. For instance, a $2.00 allowance can be given as a $1.00 bill, and the rest in dimes.

Use three banks, or three "money jars," to help your child learn the concept of saving:

- one bank, or jar, for tithe,
- one for savings, and
- one for spending.

Each week, help your child empty the contents of the tithe jar into the tithe envelope to document what they are giving. In this way, every time the child receives money, they can begin to think of giving a tenth for tithe, some to save, and some to spend.

Bible Text: Malachi 3:10, last part.

God promises to give a special blessing to those who return a tithe. He also says that there will be so much blessing that there won't be room enough to hold it all!

God's Promise

God promises to give a special blessing to those who return a tithe. He also says that there will be so much blessing that there won't be room enough to hold it all!

Activity: Have your child fill a large bowl with dry cereal, and then pour that big bowl of cereal into a smaller bowl.

Discussion: What happens when you pour the contents of the big bowl into the smaller bowl? [There is so much cereal that there is no room for it all–it overflows.]

How is that like God's blessing?

How would that make you feel to have *so* much blessing that it "overflows"?

What would you do with an overflow of blessing? [Use the cereal as an example.] What could you do with the overflow of cereal? [Share it with others, give thanks for having more than you need, etc.]

Think About This:
What kind of blessing do you think God means?
Is it money?
Is it a special closeness to God?
Is it knowing that He cares for us?
Is it special help when we need it?
In what ways has God blessed you and your family?

Suggestion: Keep a "Blessings Log" and document all the good that God is doing for the family as a result of their faithfully tithing.

A-MAZE-ING !

Directions: Can you find your way through the maze to take your tithe to the storehouse? (Careful! Don't cross any lines!)

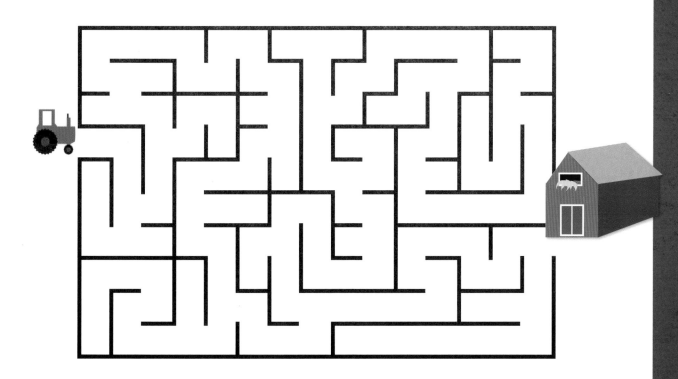

The "Giving Back" Word Search

This might be *hard!* You can ask your big brother or sister to help you.

Directions: Eight words are hidden in the puzzle below. They can go up, down, sideways, backwards–and even diagonally!

O	H	P	F	K	M	G	H	N	A
L	W	L	U	Z	T	N	A	N	R
Y	H	N	N	S	X	I	P	X	Z
D	J	W	E	F	G	R	P	P	J
G	V	N	G	R	P	E	Y	H	R
E	O	Z	X	Q	X	F	A	M	H
H	F	I	W	K	E	F	Z	G	R
Y	A	E	F	D	K	O	I	U	W
T	I	T	H	E	O	V	G	A	W
K	C	A	J	B	E	G	R	T	U

Word list:

give
God
happy
honest
Jack
offering
owner
tithe

Heart and Treasure

Directions: Break the secret code to discover a secret message from Jesus! (A couple letters are done for you to get you started.)

A	B	C	D	E	F	G	H	I	J	K	L	M

N	O	P	Q	R	S	T	U	V	W	X	Y	Z
	18								26			

"   O   W   O
 17 18 12   26 7 8 12 8   16 18 25 12

                                     ,
 23 12 8 3 24 25 12 8   20 24   23 7 8 12 8

 W   O
 26 20 22 22   16 18 25 12   7 8 3 12 23   19 8

          O."   W   6:21.
 3 22 24 18   14 3 23 23 7 8 26

Fetch These Books!

Stewardship Jack is a real dog who has a knack for teaching children about Christian living.

Meet Stewardship Jack

In his second book, *Jack and the 10 Rules*, Jack explains the Ten Commandments in simple rhymes and with charming photographs of the poodle preacher.

In the third book, *Jack's Hats*, children learn that God has given each of them unique talents and that using these gifts in His service is part of being a good steward. Children can choose to be just who God created them to be.

Are you hoping that your children will take to heart the Christian principles you value so much? Then enlist some help from a furry friend any kid would love—Stewardship Jack.

Jack and the 10 Rules
978-0-8280-2690-1

Jack's Hats
978-0-8280-2718-2

Hardcover.

Availability subject to change.

www.stewardshipjack.com

Review&Herald.

REVIEW AND HERALD® PUBLISHING ASSOCIATION | SINCE 1861 | WWW.REVIEWANDHERALD.COM